STAGE
6
BOOK 6

THE MISTAKE

John Townsend

RISING ★ STARS

Miss Evans was very stressed.

"I'm expecting a visit from the inspector later," she said. "They might close us down if we're not looking good. This room is in a mess. Can you all make Club OK look better than just OK?"

"You can depend on us," Halim grinned.

"This room needs a coat of paint," Maya sighed.

Beth cheered, "Yay, why don't we paint the walls?"

"YEAH!" Caleb gave an excited yelp.

"There are tins of bright paint and brushes in this cupboard," Miss Evans said. "I wish this bottle was an anti-stress drink instead of brush cleaner. I'm so stressed I can't even open it!"

"You're turning it the wrong way," Halim laughed.

Caleb added, "Bottle tops turn anti-clockwise."

"Listen to the experts!" Maya mumbled.

Beth groaned, "There's no non-drip white paint or rollers."

Miss Evans sighed, "I'll pop up the road and get some. We've got to do all we can to this place to impress the inspector."

Asad smiled, "I'll come with you, Miss Evans. You need a strong guy to carry stuff, while you lot work non-stop to get this place ready."

Miss Evans frowned. "Can I trust you two to behave?" she said. "I don't want any nonsense and mischief while I'm out. I want no misbehaving and I want you all to co-operate. You can start by painting the notice board with this red paint. OK, boys?"

"You can trust me — I'm your star," Halim grinned. "And Caleb's my co-star!"

Maya and Beth looked at each other and exchanged wicked smiles.

Miss Evans called from the door, "I've asked the cleaner to pop round to give the kitchen a scrub, so don't get in the way. I want this place to be spotless and sparkling within an hour."

"Just relax. We'll sort it," Halim winked.

As soon as they began painting, Beth gave Maya a wink, "I think the twins have misled us again, Maya. They're not experts at all. One of them can't even paint ..."

"That's Caleb," Halim said.

Beth giggled as she flicked red paint at him, "Now I can tell you apart. Halim has got red hair!"

It was then that the real mischief began.

Halim flicked blue paint at Beth. Maya flicked green paint at Caleb. Beth flicked red paint at Halim. Caleb flicked pink paint at everyone ... even up the wall.

Paint flew everywhere. Beth aimed at Halim but she misjudged and spattered the whole wall.

Suddenly there was a knock at the door and they froze.

"Now look what you've done!" Beth exclaimed in horror.

"It looks like an explosion in a paint factory in here," Maya gasped.

Halim answered the door.

"That's a relief," he said to the woman. "Your mop and bucket are this way."

He led her into the kitchen. The others began to clean up the mess.

Then a man knocked at the door.

Maya gasped, "Please come in and sit down. Miss Evans will be back soon. I'll ask the cleaner to make you a cup of coffee."

"But I *am* the cleaner," he said.

Beth shrieked, "That means the woman mopping the kitchen is the inspector!"

Beth ran into the kitchen, pleading, "I'm sorry, we've made a big mistake. Please let me explain … but don't close us down. Please!"

The inspector smiled, "Not at all. I love to see that everyone has to work here. That's good. But I'll tell you what I love most of all about Club OK …"